Gra

CW00918241

J. J. Merelo

JJ Merelo

This work is under a Creative Commons-Attribution-ShareAlike
4.0 license

http://creativecommons.org/licenses/by-sa/4.0/

JJ Merelo

Table of Contents

Granada Off

Granada off the beaten track, a look at the hidden treasures of the dreamed city.

By **JJ Merelo**

PROLOGUE

This is Granada On – Granada Off the Beaten Track, a set of experiences you should not miss on your third or fourth visit.

Why

When I started this book, I had been living in Granada for thirty years. Every day I walk to my day job or walk about to vent off I try to follow a new path or double a corner to a street I have never been before, I find new graffiti, a derelict house that is derelicter or a statue that very few people have seen and even less care about. And I have always thought, one day I will have to write about this, and do it in English, just because.

The title

This book might be called Granada hacks. It might still be, in some future edition. *Hacks* is the title of a series of books that tell you how to use programming languages, or whatever (there is even a Mind Hacks) in ways you had not thought about before. This book will be more or less the same. It will tell you how to live and experience and do Granada (and maybe somewhere else) in a new way.

You got me. But will you speak about the Alhambra?

I should, should I not? It is unavoidable, but there are excellent books to learn about its history and its art and its legends. So while it is going to be impossible to avoid, in principle there will be no Alhambra hack. Or maybe I should make it the first one to get it out of the way and continue with the rest.

But, again, why?

Lately I have been hanging around in Quora and they ask all kinds of stuff about Spain, Granada, and I keep answering them in a haphazard way. With this, I intend to answer and then point them to this repo and/or the Kindle book that will result from it.

Besides, this has all been an exercise of knowing thyself, or whatever equivalent of that ancient word is there for the first person. Or rather of knowing thy city. I have had to research lots of parts, which has led me to understand a bit more of the history of my city. Which is, to a point, my very own history.

But if you are asking why I am doing this in

English, when it is so not my mother tongue, well, it looked like a good idea when I started. You know, writing for expats and all that. Most tourists that come to Granada are from, you know, not here and speak in tongues.

But I guess that the main thing is that most of the material I have been using, and linking from the main text, is not in English. So, in some cases, references to facts or biographies or explanations might not be available elsewhere. So someone, eventually, might profit from this material available in English, I guess.

Last time I wrote a whole novella in English and published it managed to make all of half a dozen sales. So this one will probably fail spectacularly. I might eventually decide to translate it into Spanish. Or into better English. Whatever I find the time and will to do first. Maybe I will just huddle in a corner and cry quietly. Or go out and enjoy, once again, Granada.

Instructions for use

Granada is an old place. Like, incredi-fucking-old. It was an Iberian city, the Iberians being the tribe that populated Spain in the first millenium BC, but it has also traces of Phoenician,

Carthaginian, wow, that was hard, Roman, possibly Jewish and of course the Arab and Christian that is the one you see. There is little left of those secret origins but names: Elvira street takes its name from Iliberri, Iberian name, possibly meaning (city) by the river, and Illiberis, Roman name, taken from that. The current name is probably more related to the pomegranate fruit than to anything else, although it could be also Gar-Anat, or Hill of the Strangers or the Pilgrims in Hebrew, or maybe Karnattah or Karnattah-al-Yahud, meaning pretty much the same in "Moorish", or in Arab according to the 1911 edition of the same encyclopedia or maybe something completely different in Phoenician related to gods or kings.

If it is already difficult to narrate the origin of the name, it might be impossible to create a narrative for the city. That is why have not tried to thread the different parts of this book. I really doubt there is one, a city and the people that live in it are just there, and same as there is not a single route to visit the city, there is no single history that can be told around experiences and objects in a particular city like Granada. So after reading the tips that are in the first chapter, you can jump around from one section to the next, or read just a few lines and start exploring the city using Lonely Planet, only please come back here afterwards. If you want, of course. Use this book as a path for creating your own narrative of the city, as a conduit for having epiphanies in some lost alley or corner that will anchor your recollections and that will help you meet yourself. Because every travel can be an inner travel, if you just have the right guidance.

The text has also lots of hyperlinks inserted. If your ebook reader includes a browser, feel free to follow them in the same spirit as before. Unluckily, I have not been able to find English references for everything, but I have provided them whenever possible. They are mostly sources for what I am talking about, so if you think ""What the heck is this guy saying" by all means click on them and rest assured that the outrageous lie that is written on the page is confirmed by at least another outrageous complicit.

That does not mean that this book is not intended for actual browsing in dead tree form; that form is a good vehicle for showing your love to a dear friend who will visit Granada or who you intend to leave green with envy after your own visit to Granada. Both are valid and endorsed by this author.

I really encourage you to email me or reach out to me in Twitter for suggestions, criticism, compliments and, of course, to correct mistakes of which there must be quite a few. As a self-published author without the luxury, and also the burden, of an editor, I must rely on kind strangers to provide me with help in these matters. Only if you have acquired this book you will no longer be a stranger. You will keep being kind, I hope.

Enjoy

Go to the next page and have fun. Better if you are on site.

TIPS FOR WALKING THE CITY

In fact, these are tips that you can follow in any city of the world, but that will endow you with a certain gaze that will allow you to enjoy, read and understand the city in new ways. And I put them in no particular order.

- Look up. The details of the city are hidden in rooftops, chimneys, steeples, open windows and balconies. Hopper was inspired by what he saw from the elevated train he rode in New York, you can be inspired by flying pigeons, baroque street lights or boots hanging from a wire.

- Wander around. Never go from A to B following the shortest route. Get into alleys. Check out passages. Stop by shop windows. Turn your fear of missing out into desire to explore everything.

- Crowds are a magnet. However, they can either attract or repel. Follow crowds to see where stuff is happening. Avoid crowds for that unknown alley, right beside the main drag, where city life is actually taking place.

- Do not let anyone schedule you. Streets are not closed at night, and any city, anywhere, lives twenty four hours each and every day. Walk the quiet city at 4 AM and check out night owls and party-goers. 3PM in August might melt you straight away, but might give you the cooler part of town, where draft beers have to be downed at the speed of the golden light of the sun gilded even more as it goes through the bubbling lager.

- Use your other senses. Listen to birds, rustling of leaves, the music of people talking. Smell the air, the flowers at dusk, the scent of varnish in a carpenter shop. Taste water, and beer, and local wines. Touch the stone, feel the fabric, poke the walls.

- Do not hide behind a camera, but do not stop using it. When I visit a city for a few days, I come back with a thousand pictures. They help me remember what I did, and are a much better record of what I did there. And turn on geolocation in the device you are using for snapping pictures, they will help you even more to check what you did and when.

- There is a *me* in *time*. Traveling in company is great. But schedules have to be matched, preferences agreed, rhythms fitted. However, you do not have to do that 100% of the time. Wander around solo and you will be able to schedule yourself, put all your senses on what you are doing and stop for a picture, or one hundred, wherever you want. It might get lonely at lunchtime or you might want to share a beer with someone, but spontaneous and ephemeral friendships might be the best ones. And, as you will see in this book, whatever is ephemeral remains, while the permanent things decay and disappear.

These are some of the principles that I have followed visiting my own, and other cities. May they help you to find yourself somewhere else.

OFF LIMITS

Having an *off* in the title of a chapter in a book that also includes *off* in the title might put you *off* a little bit coming anywhere near what we are going to be talking about here.

Which is good, because that is sort of my point.

Every medium-size city includes some neighborhoods where locals, except, obviously, those that live there or have some errand to do and if so do it quickly and inconspicuously, never set their foot in. Granada has a a few of those, and could have even more if gentrification in the shape of big stores had not kicked in. Even so, there is maybe a single area that is, quintessentially, the place *not* to go, and that is the Almanjáyar quarter. The Wikipedia entry mentions that many people in Granada were there for the first time in 1983, when the Pope John Paul II gave a Mass there.

> Incidentally, I was there too, brought by
> bus from my home town, Úbeda. I just saw
> a big flat field surrounded by what I though
> were high-rises. And a guy dressed in
> white, far, far away, surrounded by many
> others dressed in primary colors. The thing

11

I remember the most from that trip is feeling pity from the guy that was peddling sandwiches on our way *back* to the buses.

You can get there fresh off the bus station. Go across the street and continue straight ahead. What you will find will be new-ish buildings, bars and convenience stores. The whole area was built starting in 1965, with some of the most conspicuous blocks, those that bear the name of the builder OSUNA, built later on, even in the 80s. Straight streets, which are used sometimes, or said to be used, for stolen car races, fuel barrels turned into hearths at night, sometimes, and people around them, and people just sitting around, doing nothing, which is only to be expected, since the unemployment rate hovers around 40%.

After all this, are you not discouraged to go there? You might even be encouraged if you have very specific needs, which, by the way, might be covered elsewhere in Granada, but there is maybe one day during the week when you might want to go there, and it is on Sunday mornings when the flea market is set up. Mind you, it is a flea market and there is not much to do other than taking a walk around the aisles, checkout out the peddlers, which, in many cases, were born a few blocks away, maybe buying something you need or something you do not need but is so dirt cheap that you cannot just refuse to buy it, and, in any case, return covered with dust. But you might get a glimpse of the people that live there, look at the heights, wander a bit, just a bit, off the garment shacks and drink a coffee in one of the bars, and you might even want to return another day and find it is not so bad as it is usually painted. Even here.

What about the other neighborhoods? In general, Granada is a safe place in a country, Spain, mostly safe, with 4 crimes for every 100 inhabitants, and that includes all kinds of crime. The most dangerous areas are those in which crowds gather and pickpockets do their thing, and those are precisely the parts of the city that you might want to visit. So, do not let any one put you off by declaring this or other place off limits, because wandering around to anywhere your feet will take you is the best way to know the city, and to know yourself through the city.

SNOW

For the average Joe-living-in-Granada, snow is something that happens up there, in the mountains. You go there from time to time, maybe once a year, maybe just when you realize your kid is seven year old and has never seen the snow, to slide down slopes using ripped plastic bags or trays or something equally dangerous. Sometimes you go just to lounge off in one of the incredibly expensive ski resort cafés of Sierra Nevada after parking your car in the incredibly expensive parking. With global warning, it is increasingly difficult to have natural snow even up there.

But down here? Not so often. One every few years. It happened yesterday, and will probably not happen for a few more years. But when it does it is all look at that roof with snow, loot at that car with snow, oh, it is stopped snowing, see you in half a dozen years.

Anyway, when it happens, there are many ways of enjoying the snow which you can only do in Granada:

- Walk up the slippery slopes in the Albayzín and fall down one, or several, times.

- A few days after, realize there is a river going through Granada and that it was not a parking lot with a somewhat big puddle.
- Take pictures of the Alhambra, which is red, with a bit of pink of top.

- Walk about in your snow attire that you could show off only when you took your kid to meet the snow a few years prior.

This chapter ends here. It need not be longer since the probability that you will actually see the snow in Granada is next to nil. So no need to spend valuable chapter space with it. Let us be done with it and proceed to the next chapter.

BROTHELS AND WHOREHOUSES

Let us be clear here. I am not encouraging you to visit *the inside* of this kind of places. You are obviously free to do so, and I will remain non-judgmental about it, but this chapter is not intended as an encouragement to the kind of behaviors that made this kind of establishments possible in the first place.

However, this is an off the beaten track kind of book. You must acknowledge that Lonely Planet does not include a *lewd* route in their otherwise excellent guides or that Fodor's gives one, two or three stars to kinky houses. So it is our turn to look at them from a cultural point of view and how they contribute to the overall image of the city. Besides, prostitution in Granada has been the topic of a book that was going to be published by a scholar in the university, although it eventually became just an article, which you can download and read yourself.

> You might want to argue against the main hypothesis of that work: that women in that trade cannot leave it because "they are addicted to money". However, the fieldwork done is really impressive.

First thing that characterizes them is neon. Since we are an old country, we do not care about this newish things that are the subject of podcasts and history books elsewhere. But most people and every truck driver in Spain knows that if that colored neon by the roadside is a milestone that indicates a place where you can get your rocks off. So to find them in Granada you will mostly have to drive and do it by night. There are a couple that are withing walking distance of the city itself, and they bear almost the same name: Don Pepe and Don José. There quite a few more if you do some perfunctory search in Google, although maybe you should not do that; however, the first one run at one particular point in time radio ads, and the second one can be clearly seen if you travel South through the freeway in a strip mall between Granada and Armilla, right next to a wok buffet, a sporting goods store, and Toys'r'us. The usual place where you can find this kind of things, in short.

Would you want to go there and take a few pictures from the outside?

> If you do it, be discrete and if some burly dressed in black guy comes up to you, run back to your car and speed away.

Well, why not? Amsterdam red-light district,

although at times looks like a Disneyfication of sexploitation, is a big attraction, the same as the Reeperbahn in Hamburg and other seedy places all over the world, including Times Square in the eighties. You can go, buy cheap sports t-shirts and then turn around the corner and sneak a picture of the neon signs, which, anywhere in the world, imply decadence and shabbiness. A seediness that might not be something to be proud of, but that can be otherwise put to work by creating alternative places to visit in the city. Which is what this book is all about.

There are also some places where you can watch the sex traders of the peripatetic variety. Which, of course, almost includes the word *pathetic* in it, so I guess it is the kind of thing that it is better to avoid completely. However, sometimes it is just impossible to do it. You walk down the street, and here you have a score of scantily clad women, separated by a preestablished and regular number of meters, and generally walking up and down the kerb to stave off the night chill. Not so long ago, when the buses stopped running in Paseo del Salón, it was one place where they could be seen; this is mentioned too in the study linked above. It is close to a park, which is a convenient place to perform the service. Empty spaces, consequences of the real estate bubble, are probably the environment of the other areas: Almanjáyar and Jaén road. However, the first area has now no vehicle traffic, except for bikes and skates, and the second has been gentrified, or rather strip-malled, with the addition of fast-food joints, a hotel and heavy traffic going to nearby malls. So it is difficult to say where they are now.

It is also impossible to say where they will be in the moment you read this. Except for the Don Pepe and Don José, which will last, with its neon signs, as least as much as the Alhambra. That cannot be said about the rest of the red light districts in Granada. In the sixties and before, it was the appropriately named <u>Jazmín, or Jasmine, street, the one that concentrated the most whorehouses in Granada</u>. And the placement of this particular zone is curious. Most tenderloin districts seem to be close to transit areas: harbors, train stations. This one is smack in the middle of the city, meters away from the city hall, and, well, army barracks. It is also very close to one of the main churches in town, the Virgen de las Angustias, a church often visited by old whores known by name: <u>la Bizcocha</u>, who according to the Spanish Nobel Prize of Literature, Camilo José Cela, was one of the most interesting characters in the city. Such an interesting character probably did not exist, as mythical creatures are wont to do: it was the name of a house in the Manigua neighborhood, right behind the back of the current police office, and by extension, the manager of the bordello that existed there until the sixties or maybe seventies.

Houses, and street, that you can still visit wandering around a quiet neighborhood absent of any kind of catcalls and covered with graffiti, which is other kind of local color. There is nothing left, because Granada is very fond of forgetting its own history, and here, "whatever is permanent vanishes, and the ephemeral remains". Which is probably bad, even if that history is, and maybe should be, forgettable.

THE ART OF THE ROUNDABOUTS.

A roundabout is a convenient way of distributing traffic among three or more roads, right? Wrong. In Spain, roundabouts have been elevated to art. First, because of roundabouts themselves. They are the way a major of a small city is telling the rest of the world, hey, check this out, this is an important place. It is so very important that we need this roundabout to distribute traffic. No more cars stopped in the middle of the roads with none, sometimes one, car waiting behind to go to important and nice places. Now *all* cars will have to either yield to none or one car or anyway brake and take a small detour and they will have MORE time to contemplate our beautiful city! Plus it will give a job to my cousin, a hard working guy, but unfortunately unemployed. And five or six other assorted citizens of this talented and hard-working town.

You say roundabout, I say pork barrel. Roundabouts have reached such proportions that some newspapers are looking for the ten ugliest roundabouts in Spain, and it was hard work, there is even a full website devoted to them, comparing the situation before and after.

The article above there are 23000 roundabouts in Spain. Fortunately, we have quite a few in Granada.

In order to enjoy them fully, the best examples are on the GR-3303 road which starts on the upper left corner of the Parque de las Ciencias, between the Tico Medina park and the BMN buildings. >I will have to write a chapter on these, too...

That road skims the outskirts of Granada, a dairy farm, and glorious examples of the art of the roundabout. But the thing about roundabouts is that once they are there, you cannot just let them become overgrown week cupolas. You have to do *something*. That something is, almost always, art. Also flags. In Spain we are fond of waving flags, and a mast with a flag is something every major is as fond of as of letting it there and not substituting even if it is now just a bunch of rags stirred by air currents. But what flag, well, that is a conundrum. You can pretty much know what political party is in power by looking at the flag. If it is a Spanish flag, that is probably the Popular Party. If it is not, well, it is any other party, but it depends. Might be the regional flag, maybe the European flag, maybe some other flag... You can see both in this roundabout tour. Or *tourabout*, first one belonging to Churriana, second to Gabias. But not only that. Art.

For instance, this sculpture, which is devoted to the victims of Franco, although you really have to look hard, and stop there, to check that they are actually fingers and not some strange mutant vegetable or creature from the underworld. But after the tribute to victims of the dictatorship, what is left to homage? Of course, the Seat 600 the car of the middle class during the self-same Franco years. But, you know, cars produce CO_2 and all that. Bad, bad for the environment. So we will also give a tribute to trees. There is no concentration of bizarre roundabouts anywhere else in the country.

Plus if you go a bit further away, to Alhendín, you can see a very small roundabout, with a bit of probably brown grass in it, that needed 14 politicians to be inaugurated. That was an absolute record, even for Spain. Or even in Granada, where there is a helicopter in a roundabout, between the road to Armilla and Camino Ronda; you can visit it right before taking the road. You say helicopter, I say hobo dwelling: someone started to live there and had to be ousted by the police. Hey, you can not

23

beat the views. >Actually, that is fake. Not the helicopter. The squatter. We love helicopter roundabouts in Granada, actually. There is another <u>with a fake helicopter in Ogíjares</u>, close to Alhendín. And sculptures.

Remember next time you see *something* in the middle of a roundabout in the suburbs of Granada. Do not ask What the heck is *that*?. The answer is always *Art*.

THE (NEARLY ABANDONED) TRAIN STATION AND OTHER TRACKS OF THE PAST

If you are in Granada, it is as likely that you arrived by train as by cruise ship. Unless you happened to be in Seville and had a lot of time in your hands plus a real love for trains, it is quite unlikely that you took that mean of transport to enter Granada. In fact, even if you did, and you did it in the last few months, you would have arrived at the train station via coach from Antequera, since the works preparing it for the AVE, the high speed train, have had it closed for the last few months of 2015.

> Despite what Paul Theroux said in The Pillars of Hercules, there is not, and has not been as far as I have been able to find out, any direct train between Málaga and Granada.

But maybe you have arrived via AVE, which would be a good sign, first because it would mean that I have eventually finished this book, and second because it would mean that the AVE railway has, indeed, arrived eventually to Granada. And you might have noticed strange signs in that trip. For most of the trip, you will

25

have the sun on your right or on your left, because it is going to be traveling south. However, when you arrive in Granada, the sun will play a trick and will change places, because you will be speeding towards the north-east. This is because the high-speed line looks like a mirror image of a J. The top will be in Madrid, the bottom of the J will be in Antequera, nicest station in the middle of nowhere, by the way, and the tail will end up in Granada. If you look at it from the other way, starting in Granada, it means that for around one hundred and odd kilometers you will be getting farther away from Madrid, not getting closer. All in all, it means that the high speed train will save half an hour, maybe a full hour, from the trip you could take in a slightly-disrespectful-of-the-speed-limits car.

There is probably a good reason for this, and there is one, or several, for the increasing neglect of the railroad in this part of Andalucía. As there must be one for the suppression of red-eye express services to Barcelona, daily services to Madrid, since there are only a couple now, and they take several hours. Once I decided to take a train from Granada to Valencia, which is a good five hours, coffee stops included, by car. It took nine hours, including a change of trains in Linares Baeza. It felt like traveling across time lines.

I guess this is why I talk about this here. There is no track that has been less beaten than the railway tracks. It is probably worth the while, if you are interested in old machinery and utilitarian buildings, to visit the station. This station was called *Andaluces*, the name of the street it is now and the name of the private company that originally built it, and it was called that way because it was one of the two stations, separated by less than one kilometer, there were in Granada

> There was probably a good reason for this too.

There is something illogical about this station, as said in a study of the stations and depots in Andalucía. Even being a terminus station, because the trains do not go any further, it is built as a bypass station, with buildings and tickets booths to one side, instead of at the end of it.

> By now, I do not need to write it myself, but here I go: There is probably also a good reason for this.

Walking along its berms, you can clearly snap pictures of the Alhambra, San Jerónimo and, to the other side, the bustle of the Camino de Ronda. It was built by the beginning of the XXth century, and although it lacks the kitsch glamour of the stations of Córdoba or Jerez, its brick buildings remind the mudéjar architecture that can be found in the Albayzín. Plus it is an empty, quiet space, where you can find abandoned buildings and wagons, if that is the kind of thing you like. Much better in this shape than what was projected for its future, a concrete monster designed by the architect Moneo which was fortunately scrapped during the crisis. Like the Estación Sur, which I never knew and which is known today mainly as the last stop for the high-speed bus line, the LAC. If you stop there, make a right and then walk along the sidewalk up to the rail bridge, you will see on the left bit brick buildings that used to house the workshops for that station. If you walk in the opposite direction and check out the outline in this article you will be able to see where the station was initially, almost on top of a small tunnel leading to the Chana quarter.

Maybe you will not. And the reason will not be that it is turned invisible, it is that it has been condemned and will probably be demolished in the near future. Which is a metaphor for the whole relationship between Granada and trains.

Maybe you will be able to see another few railway remains here and there in Granada, mainly from the light rail service that worked until the early seventies. After that, the rails remained for a time, until they were covered with asphalt or eliminated due to complains by moped and bike users; however, there ones at the crossroad between Alhamar and San Antón have been kept as a souvenir, at least while additional protests do not do away with them, like they probably did with the ones in the Málaga street.

Or you might be able to ride the spanking new light rail, also called metro although it is only underground for a few meters. However, it is been a work in progress since 2007 until the end of 2015 and there does not seem to be an end in sight. Although it has been slated to open in 2016, the segment that goes through this train station we are talking about has not been started and, if it opens, it will be in a short trip which might not be profitable and will have go the same way of other light rail systems in Jaén or Vélez Málaga: spanking new tracks and stations, but no trains running.

While that happens, the rail yard is still a great place for urban exploration. Give it a go.

HAUNTED MANSIONS

Actually, this thingie above should read mansions that should be haunted. The problem is that haunting, *per se*, does not happen. So, the the phrase that starts with "Actually, this thingie" should actually talk about mansions, houses, abodes that, when seen in a certain light in a movie, are 9 out of 10 times haunted. You know what I'm talking about: big, imposing, derelict house; boarded windows, a few nasty graffiti here and there, overgrown garden becoming a veritable ecosystems, chipped, decaying paint, and maybe lights in a window at odd times. Well, I haven't checked that last one. But I can guarantee Granada hosts a few of the others. >As does any self-respecting city, new or old. The "haunting" look is not related to age; left to its own devices, houses start to look haunted in a few year's time, as soon as the "For sale" sign decays and drops. Because capitalism, after all, goes against the grain of the spooky atmosphere.

The one that comes to mind to me immediately is the one in <u>Alamillos de San Cecilio, number 9</u>. Except for the garden, it's got all the rest. Plus stone balconies, an iron

> Iron gate! Just imagine it screeching or
> buzzing when hit by the wind, or the high
> pitch when it is opened, most probably
> with the sun setting over Sierra Elvira

gate, a stone balustrade, and a door into a windowless room. I would love to see it from inside. Except I cannot, that is why it is included in this "haunted" chapter. It would be an excellent target for urban exploration, as is the next one placed in el Barranco del Abogado, between the Camino nuevo del Cementerio and the Balcón de Granada street. It looks like the kind of condo a washed up artist would habit over in Malibu hills, but it is actually in one of the most authentic neighborhoods in Granada, wit its graffitied status reflecting the fact that it has never, and probably will never, be habited. Besides, it is a house that can be seen from all over, since el Barranco is actually a creek with houses hanging from it; its square glass hall, when hit by the sunlight just right, looks like a flying saucer landed in the slope of the hill.

It is not quite clear what is the origin of the haunting. The fact that it does not look alike any other building in the surroundings, or that maybe the overhanging balcony exceeds the habitability rates or some other public regulation might have something to do with it.

31

The fact is that it has not decayed because it is actually a great structure, concrete and iron plaques, great insulation, or maybe because it is being actively kept until the administrative logjam clears off. When it does, I can imagine it being occupied by an old glory, silver in his temples, that wakes up early in the morning to watch, glass of aged whiskey in hand, the sun rise over Sierra Nevada. In fact, watching sun rise over Sierra Nevada reflected in its glass windows is quite an spectacle.

You might want to go downhill from there and back to the Realejo, where in an unassuming and dark alley called Ballesteros you can find a whole haunted palace for yourself, the Condes de Castillejo palace. Its renaissance and facade and chamfered balcony would have a place in any touristic guide. But now it is just covered by graffiti and decaying, all by itself, until somebody rediscovers it and pays whatever it takes to un-haunt this XVI century palace, who was probably built by Siloé, one of the treat Renaissance artists in Spain and also author of the cathedral of Granada.

While it is usual enough that nobody cares about an abandoned mansion or an illegal building, it is weird enough the state of dereliction a historic palace is in, at least for a tourist mentality. Almost anywhere else in the world, Italy, France, not to mention the United States of America, a big tourist trap with dioramas and a gift shop would have been built here. Or even just a pub. A non-void. Unfortunately, this is a usual pattern in Spain, which is and maybe will always be a poor country, unable to leverage one of the resources that make the bulk of the gross national product: history. In fact, Granada depends on the Alhambra for 2.5% of its provincial income, with 70% of incoming tourists coming just to visit it. I guess that means that city honchos say, what the heck, let us just pile up on it and leave these other things to rot.

You will find many more in that area and anywhere else in Granada; there is no dearth of abandoned houses, even abandoned caves, presumably abandoned because, you know, they are caves, but there are also spectacular mansions not too far away as the crow flies, but at the other side of the river, in a alley that goes down from the end of the Cervantes Avenue known as Callejón de las Monjas. This house is called Villa Montserrat and is a delicious mixture of moorish, Central European, and a bit of oriental in the ceilings thrown in for good measure, which is said to have belonged to the

Duke of Ahumada, the founder of the Civil Guard and built by the beginning of the 20th Century. It is got a ceramic chimney of a impressive turquoise color, a tile of the Virgin of the Angustias by its main door, and stained glasses in several rooms.

The pagoda-like aspect of its roofs might or might not be the reason why a Buddhist group called The Way of the Diamond has acquired it recently for 360.000€, which seems like a incredibly good price.

> A hundred thousand euros less than that amount will not buy you an apartment just up the street, in the Bola de Oro neighborhood. So I guess this was a pretty good deal.

If you are into meditation, you might do a bit of haunting yourself in site for a fair price, although by the end of 2015 they seem to offer only workouts cleaning the space.

Haunted and also spiritual, in a way, is the Hotel del Reúma, or Rheumatism hotel, which is right by the river and in the slope of the Alhambra hill. And it was spiritual, and also in a way, since it housed, for a time, the Alhambra lodge of the freemasons, after having actually been a hotel for just a few years after its opening in 1916 under the name "Bosque de la Alhambra", or Alhambra forest. If there is a candidate for haunting or urban exploration, here is one: it was a hospital during the civil war and also used as changing rooms for plays taking place at the other side of the river. And it is completely shuttered and will probably be for years to come, since nobody cares too much about it, so it lays there, in the middle of the woods, rotting and rusting all by itself.

> More on freemasons on its very own
> chapter.

From that side of the river, look up to the Albayzín, where you can either find other haunting places or work out by just walking around, looking up, and checking out wrought iron balconies, boarded-shut windows and "for sale" signs. Places like the derelict *cármenes* in the Albayzín, the Dar-al-Horra palace, only recently opened, and, of course, the haunted apartment blocks that dot the the outskirts and suburbs of the city and that are a relic of the real estate bubble. Places you will be able to watch from outside, but never get in, specially after dark.

BUSKERS, STREET PERFORMERS, MIMES, FLASHMOBS AND OTHER STUFF MAINLY HAPPENING OUTDOORS

You might or might not find them, or by the time you read this maybe they have moved to some place sunnier and where their art is better appreciated. But there are a few recurring remarkable characters some of which I will include here for the only reason I have seen them and liked them.

The first one is, actually, the one that has compelled me to write this chapter. I met him for the first time with a big smile singing in a strange language in front of the Varagua bar, right where the *roman* bridge disembowels lots of people coming from the Zaidín, the Escolapios school, the Mercadona, and, lately, the LAC. He was playing an instrument that, at first sight, looked like a pregnant banjo but, on second thought, was probably a *kora*, which made the person using it a *griot*, or, better, a *jali*. He seemed immensely happy, smile and music not falling from his lips for the whole time I was there, and his song seemed, at the same time, a happy story but with a sad, lamenting, undercurrent.

> It is probably not a kora, but a N'Goni.
> However, it is nearly impossible for me to
> make out the differences between them.

Later on I watched *El ritmo de la calle* (The street beat), where he is featured along with many other street musicians of all kinds and origins. His name is Ibrahim Diakité, and he apparently lives in Granada. In fact, I saw him again in the self same place, by the end of November 2014, happily beating his kora and swinging his spiky hair and foot to the rhythm of his music, by himself, almost, but not quite, oblivious of the autumn that was settling him all around him. And, if you happen to miss it, you can always watch him in this YouTube video. Where can you find him? It is difficult to say. Not the kind of job you do nine to five in a fixed place, but according to my own experience and videos found (like this one) either in Paseo de los Tristes, right in front of the Alhambra, or by the roman bridge, at the beginning of el Paseo del Salón.

That is not an usual place for buskers, although it is quite usual to find umbrella and trinket peddlers there. You will have to move a few hundred of meters up, to Puerta Real or up the Carrera de las Angustias, which have become

Busking Central. Of late not many musicians are there, but there are mimes galore. The one that seems to be suspended off a broomstick, the sad silver witch, and, sometimes, and that is not busking, the roast chestnut seller, and the Disney characters that sell balloons or maybe get paid for posing in pictures. The esplanade in front of the fountain is where you can find sometimes groups such as Elsa Bhör. Puppets and string quartets set up their act by the left hand side of the Isabel la Católica, in the pedestrian lane that goes up to Ángel Ganivet, and if you keep walking up Reyes Católicos, you will arrive to Plaza Nueva, where big acts such as *batucadas* or even flamenco cry and dance in front of the many tourists that are there. They are probably the less authentic and more tourist-oriented acts, but they are worth a while anyway. Other groups like El mundo del revés usually work their reggae tunes further down the street, in the Paseo de los Tristes.

The problem is Granada is that we are fond of forbidding things. The mime is sad because she cannot mime. Begging is OK, miming is off-limits. So she puts her makeup every weekend but can just stand there, waving sad hellos or goodbyes and waiting for someone to drop an euro in her silver hat. Music has been banished from the Albayzín, maybe because too much of a good thing can be as bad as too little.

Like this chapter, that has been too much on the beaten track, since buskers ply their trade wherever crowds gather and can be parted with their spare change. However, it departs the beaten track of historic anecdote and old stones to focus on listening and watching people. People so ephemeral, that, as is so often said of Granada, they are permanent.

CASTLES IN DANGER

Spain and Granada have got their share of McMansions and what we could call suburban kitsch. During the early 2000s, the real estate bubble created big developments from places where only shrubbery was found before but, in some cases, it did not do it fast enough and got caught by the bubble bursting.

Peligros, which literally means Dangers, is a small city at the North of Granada; somebody decided that castles would look great in mockups and in real estate leaflets and built a whole street of them. You can see the twin towers from the sky, two whole rows of them, with swimming pools acting as moats only they are on the back and they would defeat no enemy other than decaying property values and, pun intended, underwater mortgages.

They actually are, at least this year, in the middle of nowhere, as if they were going to stand a siege, surrounded by neat streets with neat names but almost no houses. That is great for parking space and probably for creating great infancy moments, but probably not for garbage collection and, again, property values.

At street level they do look impressive if abandoned, most windows shuttered, almost no sign of actually having been occupied. Nice view to the snowy mountains, too. Just imagine waking up in your tower bedroom (which, by the way, must have been a feat to heat) and holding a cup of mead, looking at the distance and thinking "Yes, I am the sire of all my sight can reach". Or maybe "How I will be able to make mortgage payments with these huge utility bills?". Whatever.

> This chapter was inspired by a tweet by Ferminius, who is a great person and photographer. He captures Granada like few others, so you will do well by following him in any social media.

FAST FOOD

You already know about *tapas*. They are (usually) fast enough, although the racket is to take enough bringing the tapa so that when it arrives you are already done with your bear and you order the second. And then they can skimp on the last one. Happens all the time, just do not go back to the place and bash it in Tripadvisor.

Besides that, there are several local equivalents of fast food joints.

> And I do not mean here local pizza or donuts or cronuts or wok franchises. I mean the real deal, born and raised in Granada.

However, let me tell you something about the *tapas*. They are not fast. At all.

And it is like that for a good reason. Just look at the economics of the free tapa with the drink. Look at the costs. The beer is almost free. And it is like that for several reasons. Most bars stock a single or a couple of different beers on tap, it has a high rotation. It is served in bite sizes: the *caña* is 1/5 or 1/6 liters, or 1/3rd if you ask for a

42

tubo, but the cost of the liquid itself will hover around 10 cents.

This means that when you are buying a drink, you are actually paying for the tapa. The tapa also has the most added value. But also the cost. This means that if you skip a tapa you will be paying the two odd euros for something that costs a few cents.

That is why tapas are not so fast. Mind you, they are faster than a proper sit down meal. But it is in the interest of the (mean) bar owner to extend as much as possible the period between serving the beer and actually serving the tapa.

Plus tapas are usually salty and greasy things that give you thirst. And they arrive at the tail end of your glass of beer, so very often you will order *another* beer when the tapa for the first is arriving to chase it down.

This means that you have to choose and choose well when you want you Spanish fast food to be really fast, and not slightly-faster-than-very-slow. Fortunately, there are many places like that in Granada.

And then there are the genuine local fast-food joints, places that serve sandwiches and that will get you fixed in no time, as long as you do not mind to eat standing up and with minimal support for your beer and elbows. In fact, since these places are usually less crowded, and more accessible, that the MacKings and Montana Fried Turkeys, it is the place to go before going to the theater, yes, we have that from time to time in Granada, or to the movies or if you have the munchies any time of the day. Places like the Frankfurt's Bocanegra, with several types of hot and cold sandwiches and show cooking, which means that the grill is right there and you can watch your beacon simmer while you sip, just a bit, your beer. Places like Bar Aliatar with many types of sandwiches, most of them based on pork, or Bodegas la Mancha, where you can taste an artichoke sandwich which will make you want to turn vegetarian. Not me. I hate artichokes. But since you are reading this book by a no-name dude, you are probably open to new experiences, so you will probably want to do that.

Good thing about this is the cost: less than five euros for a sandwich plus the beer. Depending on the sandwich, you will have some change left for coffee. Which you will want to take elsewhere, of course.

WATER

I did not intend to make this (book,pamphlet,guide,loose collection of words ← choose one or several or none) a sensory experience with all, or a few, senses explored in their very own chapters. In fact there is a old Spanish ditty that goes

```
Dale limosna, mujer
Que no hay en la vida nada
Como la pena de ser
Ciego en Granada
```

Loosely translated as

```
Yo, woman, give him the alms
Because there is nothing in life
Like the sorrow of being
A blind man in Granada
```

It would be also a real pity if you did not have the pleasure of tasting tap water in Granada. And this fact is something I have found rather late in life. Many people prefer the water they have palated in their hometown, the place where they were born. But in Úbeda, were I was born and raised, water carried so much lime that taps had to be routinely cleansed and showers dug out of the calcareous agglomeration they carried. Even so, it was not like I was getting out of Úbeda and saying, every time I drank a glass of water, "Hey, this is the stuff".

But that is exactly what happens to me when I get out of Granada. Really. The first time you stop at a roadside café, two hours into foreign territory, and, it is all "what the hell, they call *this* water?".

> Except in Vienna. They have wonderful tap water there. So wonderful that they created a monument to it right in front of the monument to the soviet soldier that they wanted to hide. But that is a completely different story. They also have excellent tap water in Iceland, if you let it flow for a good while after having used hot water and the sulphur smell and taste that goes with it.

Tap water, everywhere in and around Granada, is really good. It is cool and fresh and does not have the usual tang of chemicals used in purification. Plus it is really safe. Mostly everywhere in Europe, really, but the taste and flavor will vary. It is really much better than most *el cheapo* bottled water and it comes very close to Lanjarón bottled water since, in fact, they come from pretty much the same source.

I guess the trick is that it comes fresh from the reservoirs that take water directly from Sierra Nevada. In Canales, which you can visit and I encourage you to do so, it is a few kilometers away from Granada and close to Güéjar Sierra, nice place to eat and to just be,

> It is also the reason why, or one of them at least, why there are no tram from Granada to the Sierra. That, too, is a different story.

and Quéntar water does not have a long run from the snow and ice of the Sierra, so it is pristine when it, eventually, arrives to your glass.

You will not probably be able to take it home, because it will be dutifully requisitioned by the airport rent-a-cops, but its taste, or complete absence, is something that will linger on your tongue for a long time. Guaranteed.

ECCENTRICS AND ODDBALLS

If you are looking for somebody a bit odd among the *normal* citizens of Granada, you might not need to go further than yourself, even more so if you are wearing a cap with the bill sideways, flowery shirt open at the front, and the biggest eccentricity of them all: socks and sandals.

However, I am not talking about yourself, or not only about yourself, in this chapter. Not about the kind of person that ends up with his very own Wikipedia page, although some of them, like Ángel Ganivet, were the kind of person that dives into a frozen river when they are far away from home. There are characters in the narrative of a city that, due to its presence in many acts, eventually become part, if not archetypes, of the city itself. These are the holy fools of yore and, nowadays, just people that you might know by name but, above that, by its behavior and the eccentricity that defines them. That is why I will not use their name, even if I know it.

Let us call the first one Randy, since he has got a vague similitude to the big philosopher and thinker Randy Hickey, brother of Earl and sidekick in his adventure to restore his karma. Big and balding and sometimes using suspenders, his real name matches that of one of the saints that protect Granada. He can be seen around tapas time in the city center, wearing suspenders, and asking for cigarettes. Sometimes picking stuff around in bars to see if there is some spare change to pick up or is treated to a beer, or smoking, if he already got one. He is mostly inoffensive, he can scare you off nonetheless by bumming cigarettes in a loud voice and unannounced. And he can be dangerous in the presence of girls, so beware.

We can call the next ones *the rosemary ladies*, since, indeed, I have no idea how they are called and they change from time to time, plus rosemary twigs are their weapon of choice. These are the women that offer you a rosemary twig near the entrance to the cathedral and, when you extend your hand to pick it up, grab your hand and start to read it as if they knew how to do that kind of thing, telling you obvious things, or not so obvious, and then requesting five or ten euros, depending on whether your look American or just the backpacker kind of tourist. They are not dangerous, but they can yell curses at you from a long distance, so better dodge them when you find them.

We also have our share of winos, which in Spain either drink openly from liter bottles of beer or sip from tetrapaks of supermarket plonk. For some reason, they gather around the Plaza de la Trinidad, at the tip of Paseo del Salón close to the bridge and also in Plaza Nueva. They fight sometimes, but they more pitiful than dangerous.

And on the other side of the law and among Granada's finest, a policeman that went by the alias of Pavarotti for no reason other than his having a beard, became also famous for his whistle. Traffic in Granada is notoriously deadlocked, and he used a special-order whistle to put a bit of order in that chaos. Only he apparently did it too much and too early, and some law professional living in the neighborhood took a notary home to measure the noise level and eventually sued him. It came to naught, but the local daily, the Ideal, received more than 30 letters to the director either loving or hating it.

> I can say myself he is a great professional. He was witness in an accident where a city bus ripped my rear-view mirror, and offered his help. When the insurance company came eventually around asking for his testimony, all was fixed and I got my car fixed.

He was eventually decorated in 2008, although later on he did not follow a strike along his colleagues and he was accused of scabbing and his gun stolen. He is probably still working, although his whistle has not been heard for some time now.

Historically, there have been other curious characters. The sometimes called *Llorica*, sometimes *risicas*, that is, either crybaby or smiley, was a beggar that worked the city center crying out, or maybe laughing, his hunger. I actually do not remember having ever seen him, but he has left his mark in several literary journals. Many of these characters have been immortalized as *cabezudos*, or big heads, in the *Tarasca* parade that takes place during the Corpus Christi. Birolio, Chorrojumo, Paniolla, are all represented as big heads during that procession, with no one being the wiser. In fact, I have watched that parade for years and was never aware of the history of those heads and how it related to real persons. Most of them have a sad history behind, being simply famous due to their presence and catchphrases, like "Pan y olla", "bread and cooking pot", which was the sentence uttered by one of them. They are also living memory, having lived during the 50s and 60s. I guess there is no other place in the world that honors its street dwellers that way. Just imagine, it is as if San Francisco honored with a fourth of July float Norman the Emperor. This is a doubtful honor, since these cabezudos walk the edges of the parade hitting kids with inflated pig bladders, but at least makes them permanent, as most ephemeral things in Granada eventually become.

Last but not least, there is a big university in Granada. There are nearly four thousand professors there, so you can expect eccentrics and oddballs galore. In order to experience them, you will have to sign for a course, which I encourage you to do, because it is the way thousands of people have experienced the city every year. You can then skip classes and just go to the Erasmus parties, since it is also the only way thousands of students have experienced the city every year.

> And I am not saying every single Erasmus student parties hard and does nothing else. There are more than a thousand students every year, so there is that kind, also the kind that parties hard and works hard, and then the kind that just works hard. Only this one is less noisy and keeps to itself, so the kinds noticed are the other two.

THE BEST UNIVERSITY IN GRANADA
There is only one university in Granada. So
that thing above is a joke. Laughs accepted;
in fact, they are compulsory. Thanks.

Granada is an university city, thanks mainly to
the UGR, which is one of the biggest in Spain
and includes more than fifty thousand students.
In a city with five times that population, that
implies that Granada lives and breathes through
its university. And that is literal in a sense:
almost 5% of the provincial income stems from
the university and eleven thousand jobs, which
is 3.5% of the total employment in the province.

And that has happened for some time now,
being also one of the oldest universities in
Spain, so this is bound to have an impact on the
city landscape. However, most of it is *in* the
beaten track.

So, off the top of my head, and outside that in-
the-beaten track fact that some buildings are
old and Gothic and venerable, university
buildings are great resources for a couple of
things: WiFi and lavatories.

In fact, I am big fan of universities
everywhere for the sanitary services they

provide. When touristing, I always follow the old adage "Pee when you can, not when you want" so if you pass by an university building, just walk confidently in and look for the lavatories, in the corridor straight ahead and to your left.

Other than that, why would you want to go to the university? For starters, it might go to you instead. There are several campus and then independent buildings. Ciencias, for instance, is in a big campus called Fuentenueva which is close to the city center. Two faculties, Translation and Law, are independent, and old, and nice, buildings very close to downtown and the other monuments. Other campus, Aynadamar houses the closely related Fine Arts and Computer Science, while Cartuja houses the also closely related Pharmacy, Psychology, marketing and humanities. The recently built Health campus includes several high rises where Nursing and Medicine is taught, as well as a big, and so far unfinished, hospital, the morgue and several research campuses. It is really unlikely that you end up, by mistake, in the Faculty of Sports Sciences, but if you visit the Gothic structure of the Hospital Real, you can be seen from the windows of the university president office.

The university cafeterias are also good reasons for visiting any of them. The *café con leche* is awful but also awfully cheap, and there is great, funny and knowledgeable company. Every one of them has a library where old and dusty tomes are housed, and you can go through while you hide from the heat or if you actually are looking for a particular book. Check out the catalog in advance. Places like the Fine Arts library or the Letters and Humanities house a good amount of contemporary literature and essays.

Plus you might want to go because they house some jewels that are missed because they are, just like the rest of this book, off the beaten track. Check out, for instance, the Cartuja Campus. It hosts, except for pharmacy, mostly non-science or engineering degrees, and you can notice the atmosphere is much more relaxed and corridors much more crowded that the ones in Ciencias or Computer Science. If you are into interminable discussion that start with coffee and end somewhere you do not really know how you got, this is your place. Besides, their cafeterias, being on a hill, offer some of the best views in Granada. The one in the Faculty of Psychology has one of the best sunsets in Granada, plus excellent company. The Faculty of Economics has also an excellent outdoor terrace with very nice views of the city. And the cafeteria in Pharmacy is in a school with one of the highest female rate and, at the same time, the highest number of students in Granada. From there, the Odontology and Communications schools share the Colegio Máximo, originally a Jesuit novitiate, but now a monastery-like place with old printing machines in the corridors, low cost dental clinic and also a beautiful neomudéjar chapel that you will probably be able to visit if you ask nicely in reception; it is completely empty but its moorish revival decoration, stained glass windows and shell-like baptismal font are really remarkable and could be an incredible background to a rave party. The whole building, even if not ancient, is remarkable and was one of the first Jesuit buildings in the area that eventually included a lot. If you are *in* the beaten track and visiting the Cartuja, which is five hundred meters away, take a small detour and visit this place too.

Because there is art here, and Art with a capital A. The university holds contests for rewarding the art of its best students, and the prize is being a part of the Modern Art Collection of the University of Granada. If there is an index to that collection, I have been unable to find it. However, having been involved with the university for a few years, I know that paintings, photographs and sculptures end up in offices, corridors and stairs anywhere. There are three in the free software office, and feel free to come and appreciate them. We would happily give them to you, since they leave us a bit like this :-?, uncultured geeks as we are, only we cannot, because they are art and belong to the humankind in general, not me or you. In fact, of those pieces of art that looked like a irregular block of concrete with jagged iron bars coming out from it spent a long time as an ashtray in the old Computer Science school. The staff had to specifically instruct the cleaning crew to neither use it as a dustbin or carry it to a dumpster as a piece of debris. Which, I guess, eventually became since it disappeared one day, not to be seen again.

I am not saying that there are not incredibly talented master works; it is quite clear that all of them are. Only since I have not been able to find a catalog except for this one, which apparently lists only more classic works and not the modern ones, I cannot point out which ones are good enough for you or where they are, my dear reader.

If you walk into the administrative area of close to the lecture halls you will be unable to avoid the pictures with the former deans, dressed with the classic university attire, one that I have been unable to avoid just once, during a Honoris Causa celebration. Just so you know, the color of the band, which for some reason is called beca, same name as for grants in Spanish, depends on the degree or maybe doctorate you obtained. I go with blue, I think, although I am not sure, since blue is for Sciences and I am actually in an engineering School. Never mind. These guys will be looking their best with academic robes. I leave as an exercise for the reader to find out which is the dominant age and genre and how it varies from one Faculty to the next one.

Because every Faculty has its own little world and is not so much a cross section of the Spanish society as a sample of a particular intellectual, attitudinal and economical status. Check out Medicine, for instance, which is now housed in its very own white high rise, one you can see from the ring road. It needs an almost perfect grade to enter, close to 99%. It is the creme of the crop coming out of high schools in Granada which you can see there. Check out Fine Arts, too. Or Sports Sciences. They have to pass an special exam, besides requiring high grades in their A-levels, or Selectividad, which is its equivalent in Spain. We even have a

Theology school, which, to tell you the truth, I have never visited. But back to Fine Arts, it is really worth a visit. Their library is excellently stocked with all kinds of media and arts texts. The building was a former madhouse built at the turn of the century, although the reforms and decoration include a couple of graffiti walls on the back. If you are in need of art supplies, it has a *economato* or student store where you can buy all kind of brushes, drawing pads and stuff needed for artistry. Its main building has an exhibition space used for works of arts by students and faculty.

> And once you are there, you can walk up the street to the other side of the roundabout and visit the ETSIIT, an important part of the geek chapter. Or use it as a warm-up to know about graffiti in Granada, since Fine Arts is at its core.

For political consciousness and painted slogans on paper rolls, check out political science or philosophy. There are always political assemblies or organized protests going on there. But if you are more into economics, check the ecosystem that has evolved around the Faculties. Having a sparse campus has spread the wealth it brings to the city and there are all kinds of shops that cater to students: bookstores, cafés, copy shops, supplies... If you walk to the Architecture School, which is in the middle of El Realejo, <u>a former military hospital and house of the Admiral or Aragón built in the XVI century</u>, which lots of people in the region remember because it was where young ones with the age to serve where parked when they alleged some kind of ailment to be rid of the military service, has evolved from a bleak and drab barrack to a <u>functional, bright and light building that has received an architecture price</u>, which is turning a former traditional and touristic neighborhood into a vibrant student area. Architecture, with its grim job outlook, accompanies now the Modern Languages Center, which is not strictly University but university-owned.

> Yes, it is complicated. But never mind, it quacks like an university, so let us let it be.

This place is the closest to an American-style college you will find here, mainly because the bulk of its students, coming here to learn Spanish, hail from the United States. That means flip-flops any time of the year, Jansport backpacks, and walking Styrofoam cups from coffee-to-go places that cater precisely to this crowd and nobody else, since any self-respecting Spaniard will have a proper sit-down coffee with olive-oiled toast on the side.

And probably the best place in the university to have one is the cafeteria in the Faculty of Law. It opens to the Botanic Garden so you can sip your capuccino and enjoy the sights, too. Besides, this is the oldest university building in Granada, if you exclude the Madrassa or Islamic University by the side of the cathedral, which you might or might not want to do if you want to make this university the oldest in Europe or not. The botanic garden itself was created in the XIX century as a subject of study. Just look at the tallest tree, which is a Ginkgo biloba, the only one in the province for a long time, or look back to the building itself, that houses the university from pretty much the same time. It was built in the XVI century and called Colegio de San Pablo. It was a school belonging to the Jesuits and one of the main centers for Latin studies in Granada, another example, as the Colegio Máximo, of the university taking over from the Jesuits, and a continuity note since current students use Latin too to say stuff like "Habeas Corpus" and "Gaudeamus Igitur". Some of them, at least.

Finally, for a glimpse of he future visit the gleaming and spanking new Biosanitary campus, which started to be used at the beginning of the first semester of the 2015-2016 course. It is white, it has high-rises, and the faculty hated it.

It was too far away from their clinics and home offices, it did not have enough parking space, it had a single bus line going through it. It does have nice light rail stations, but no actual light rail. So no joy. Be that as it may, it is now working and surrounded by research centers and weed-filled empty lots, so it kind of looks like the kind of place zombie fighters might go looking for a cure in a post-apocalyptic world. For the time being, that is. And a famous graffiti artist,

More on him on its very own chapter

Niño de las Pinturas, was commissioned to paint all its utility shacks. It is worth a visit just for that reason.

In fact, it can be the starting point for a interesting graffiti route.

ASSORTED GEEKERY

Geeks travel too. And when we arrive to some place we are, sometimes, less interested in watching old stones than in tech meetings, little museums with engineering feats, or science related places.

> I remember, for instance, seeing and playing a Theremin in a small electricity museum in Barranco, Lima. That was the only time I have been able to do so. Air and space museums in Madrid, war museums in Poland, Vienna and London, all those, are kind of really *off* the beaten track and also in the suburbs, because there are only so many places downtown where you can squeeze a few tanks and a bomber plane.

We have that in Granada, starting with the behemoth Parque de las Ciencias, which is the subject of jokes for its constant expansion, filling now more than a park, a whole block. You can very well spend the whole day there, spending half day in the temporal exhibitions and then proceed to the rest: the aviary, planetary and many other things ending with *ary*. Really a nice place and a source of learning if you can just stand the yelling herds of kids

63

that abound there. Also, since budget is always kind of tight, a showcase for retro computing if there was one: check out some of the vintage IBM and Apple computers that are the engines of some of the rides, which, in some cases, have not been upgraded since the nineties. Why should they? They work as a charm.

Unbeknownst to most people, including probably 90% of the people in Granada, the first science museum was created in a high school, and it is probably still there. It is the science museum of the Padre Suárez institute.

> The *Padre Suárez", or father Suárez, that gives his name to the institute was, you guessed it, a Jesuit that died in the XVII century. He was mainly into philosophy and he was born in Granada. Another example of the curious relationship between Jesuits and science by way of a science museum housed in a building that bears his name.

By the time you read this, it might or might not be open, although you can request a visit in his web site. The domain that hosted its pages is for sale and it has had to move to BlogSpot, and the person in charge of it retired, with the Ministry of Education not relieving any of his colleagues from classes. So it might be shuttered and gathering dust by now, another example of permanent things disappearing while the transient stays. If you manage to find it open and somebody willing to give you the spiel, there are four rooms filled with stuffed animals, mockups, physics and chemistry instruments and something called Dr. Kagerah's boxes, which is so much like the title of a terror movie that you totally have to go and check it out. If you do not make it into the building, this Flickr gallery might give you an idea of what you are missing, like this, er, oriental royal XIX century bong.

Sorry about the lighter note of that paragraph above, I really cannot help it, but it is really serious that this scientific and technical patrimony will go missing. Besides, the institute was the first one in Granada, built in the 1840s, and some outstanding citizens like Francisco Ayala, Ángel Ganivet, Asunción Linares, Elena Martín Vivaldi and Federico García Lorca. Asunción Linares was, in fact, the first woman to become professor in Sciences in Spain and only the second one after the Civil War. So, there you go. The museum was quite useful for awakening scientific consciences, and in this era where we need so many STEM graduates, even more.

But let us ride the LAC to go back to the big

science museum brother, and as you get out it, you can proceed to the so-named "Rotonda del Helicóptero", or "Helicopter roundabout", which you cannot miss since there is a helicopter there, set up on a rotating axis that makes it look this and that way, depending on wind and ground vibration. It is placed on the way to the Armilla air base, wing 78 of the Spanish Air Force, precisely the wing that flew it until not so long ago, well into this millenium. This is mainly a training wing but also houses the patrulla ASPA, a helicopter aerobatics team that features the new Eurocopter, one of just half a dozen in the world. However, there are only a few scheduled acts if you want to watch them.

> I remember to spend the time of boring classes during the 80s watching the Bucker 131 biplanes sputtering in the sky, in front of the Facultad de Ciencias. They were true relics of the 20s, and probably the ones that were used to train by current fighter pilots in the Spanish air force.

That helicopter is an Sikorsky S-76C Spirit or HE24 in SpAF denomination, was acquired in 1991 and used mainly for instrumental training in the wing, although it could be used also for ferrying people or rescue missions. It is one of the most modern helos in the SpAF, so I do not really understand what is the deal with it. Maybe it was originally bought second hand or something. You can see it in action in this video and check its former locations in this helospotters database

>Last annotation is mine, I guess. The page
>did not mention it was retired from service.

Actually, the previous location was the aforementioned Parque de las Ciencias, where apparently went after the engine broke, according to a tweet. And it was placed there to celebrate the centennial of aviation in Spain. Curiously enough, the plane was called S-76 to celebrate the *bicentennial* of the US. So, two centennials in a single decorated roundabout. This helicopter has also got a much geekier version, the S-76 Shadow, with an awkward-looking but coolly operated through a Heads-Up Display front-mounted single-pilot cabin. And that is a sentence with a lot of dashes.

>More about roundabouts in its very own
>chapter.

If you continue in the direction of the Avenida de América, past the exit of the underground tunnel, where, who knows, you might even see a train coming or going, past the nano-Manhattan by the end of that avenue, with a couple of tall buildings, and then, when you arrive at the boulevard with the frayed flags, take a left and you will arrive at the Instituto de Astrofísica de Andalucía, IAA or Andalusian Astrophysics institute. You cannot miss it, it is the one with the rocket protruding out of its front garden. It is quite an open place where you can pop in and ask someone about the Rosetta mission or about exoplanets, since this institute includes discoverers of one of the first ones. Instruments for spatial missions are created here, and there are a few on display. The rocket, for instance. It is an atmospheric research probe which was designed here and launched in the eighties, starting our regional space race.

> In this interview, José Manuel Vílchez
> mentions Manuel Merlo Vallejo, a Jesuit
> that was in the origins of the current
> Institute. Another case of Jesuits going
> hand in hand with science in Granada.
> More on this on the chapter about the
> university.

From there it is just a short stretch to the Paseo de la Bomba, which you cannot miss if you are into big steam machines, or into steampunk.

> You might take a detour to check out the
> "haunted" mansion not so far from there,

described in the chapter on hauntings.

Despite its name, which might or might not be due to a bomb falling there in the civil war or maybe to the fact that there was a big pump for the *Acequia Gorda*, or big irrigation ditch or maybe to the <u>fountain at the beginning which doest not look at all like a bomb</u>; *bomba* means either *bomb* or *pump* in Spanish, and the big machine is the roundabout could be a steam-operated pump, but is actually a press belonging to a sugar-producing *ingenio* or "engine", which is what sugar mills were called at the beginning of the Century, when high sugar prices brought unknown wealth to many countries and regions in the world, including Granada. The machine was produced in 1905 by <u>Fives-Lille</u>, a company which was also in charge of building railways all along eastern Andalucía and the lift inside the Eiffel Tower. Surprisingly, this company endures to this very day, although under the name of Fives. All steampunks should know about this company, responsible for lots of iron bridges and scary-looking machines in Andalucía.

> If you align yourself with the axis of the steam engine and look uphill, the street just in front is the Cuesta del Molino, and houses a small museum devoted to Ángel Ganivet, whom we met for the first time

above as a student of the Padre Suárez high school. But the geeky highlight is right to the left hand side of that street: an alley called "Ingeniero Ricardo de la Cierva", or Ricardo de la Cierva, engineer. Well, as far as I have been able to discover, there was no engineer called Ricardo de la Cierva. There were two Ricardos de la Cierva: one politician, killed by the republicans in the civil war, and one writer, mainly about history, and mainly attacking the republicans and pro-Franco. There were two Juanes de la Cierva, however. The first one, Juan de la Cierva y Codorniú, *was* an engineer, brother of Ricardo, and discoverer of the autogyre. Second one, Juan de la Cierva y Peñafiel father of the first Ricardo, was another politician. And there is even a third one, Juan de la Cierva y Hoces, who was the first Spaniard to receive an Oscar in 1970; he was the son of the second Ricardo and nephew of the first, and most famous, Juan de la Cierva. And he was kind of an engineer, too, since he created an optical stabilizer for cameras called Dynalens, which was used for the first time in the movie "Tora, Tora, Tora!", whose patent was registered in the US in 1973. Well, this does not belong to Granada, but it is geek and cool and

Spanish, so please admit the detour. Besides, my campaign in Twitter to acknowledge the error in the name of the street might have succeeded by the time you read this, so it might have his name or the one of a pop singer, who knows. If my change.org petition succeeds, it will have the name of Juan Montserrat Vergés, whom we mention in the chapter on freemasonry, and maybe on the one on modernist Granada, if I get to write it eventually.

This machine, along with the modernist mansions in the city center and the Gran Vía, are testimony of that era when Granada depended on a different monoculture. In this case, this machine was part of the *azucarera* San José, which was placed exactly, or rather pretty much, in this place, maybe a bit North of that, since to the South-West, where there is a wood-paneled building now, there was a tram depot for the railway line that made the trip to the Sierra, and by Sierra in Granada we mean Sierra Nevada, the sierra par excellence. This tram was dismantled in the early 70s, to never come back until now. Or maybe 2016. Who knows.

That tram was, for some time, placed in la

<u>Facultad de Ciencias, or Faculty of Sciences, of the University of Granada</u>. It might or might not be there by the time you read this, since it was taken for restoration and has not returned. However, there is another steam engine parked there and you can always check <u>the building itself</u>, which was projected and built in the sixties although it has had lots of additions. There is some fodder for geeks inside the building, where all kind of sciences, from Physics to Geology, are studied. To the right hand side, the Physics building houses a Foucault pendulum, and going from there to the main building, the library to the right hand side houses scientific journals from early on, the fifties and even before that. I have spent there a good part of my studies in the eighties, and I was elated to find an article by Einstein himself, published in the fifties in some Physics journal. Quite an interesting, if a bit over the top of my head, reading.

The main hall has all kind of widgets: rockets, other engines, maybe some other temporary exhibitions, and, from there on, the biology building has a rather creepy stuffed animals vitrine, and the geology departments all kind of rocks. There is nothing but people in the Maths area, and in the Chemistry little but pungent smells.

If you go across the parking to the next building and ask nicely, you might be able to visit Alhambra, our very own supercomputer, which is not open to the public but there will probably be someone proud enough in computing services of the University to show it to you. That is the precise building where the ur-geeks of the eighties spent our time, because it housed the first computer lab, filled with IBM XTs, and where you had to dress nicely, no shorts, if you did not want to be expelled by the janitors. This building housed the university mainframes for some time, and it still has a big data center.

If you want to see one of those computers, you will have to catch the SN3 bus to the ETSIIT, which is a geek place if there is one in Granada. You cannot miss the stop: where the nerd-looking guys get down, that is the place

> It is by a park, just in case there is a nerd glut the particular moment you ride the bus and they stop somewhere else.

The main hall is graced by a big IBM mainframe, together with all its peripherals: disk drum, data entry console, all the rest. But it did not belong to the University, but to some pioneering computing company in Granada called *Centro de Cálculo de Granada*, which has completely vanished.

Then, walk up two floors to the Department of Computer Technology and Architecture,

> Once you are there, go to the next to last office on the right on the corridor to your left, you might recognize the name of the person there, and if he is in, he will happily sign your copy of this book, or your Kindle or other reading device. Appointment not necessary.

To the right of the entrance door there is a vitrine with the history of computing as seen from the department. You can see there from *portable* computers from the early 90s, through all kind of peripherals, including a hand scanner that belonged to me, to chips that were designed from scratch in our very own department. All of it neither catalogued, nor labeled, nor acknowledged. We do not even know if it works or not, and it is closer to a storage closet than to a real museum. However, maybe some time from now, maybe even by the time you read this, someone with an interest in retro computing will use it for a master's degree project or a PhD. Or just out of spite, to give it a big of dignity.

When you get out of the building, you might want to visit the biggest data center in Andalucía, the Cloud Center Andalucía.

> Incidentally, you will go past one of the establishments we talked about in the chapter on whorehouses, the Don Pepe. None are too far, so using a pit stop as an excuse to be there is not an option.

You will not be able to see anything from outside, other than the ditch that connects it to the railway, a few meters away, where the fiber actually goes. But you can request a visit and you will be able to see the watertight rooms where all the racks are stored, the firefighting measures, and the hum of twenty-first century computing all around you. Which is something all geeks love and crave.

> Visits are only available under requests, and then only for a good reason and in a group. So you might want to gather at least half a dozen of friends to do it, and request it well in advance.

Once you are on a ride, double back and take the freeway around Granada in the Southern direction until you arrive to the "Armilla" exit. The offramp is a balcony onto the Don José, the other funhouse we have mentioned in its chapter. Right across the freeway there is a big, blue, glass building with the name Axesor on top, surrounded by other tech-related buildings in what we could call a Silicon offramp, which is a nano version of a Silicon Valley. Anyhow, Axesor is an interesting place, being one of the first pure-play Internet outfits in Spain. It was a long shot by five friends with Physics and other degrees, who decided to create a new company using new tools, the tools of the Internet that was, right them, blooming in Spain. They started as a company giving commercial information, kind of a Spanish Lexis-Nexis, but evolved to the point that it is now one of the first credit rating agencies in Spain.

Once again, not much to see there. You will have to ask for an appointment and then probably a commercial person will give you the lowdown. If you peek into the building, you will see lots of desks with computers and people busy with it. They have an interesting data center and also very exciting credit prediction technology.

> And I know this because we were the origin
> of that technology through a contract
> between them and our university.

But algorithms do not a high visual impact, although they have have all kind of other impacts when your company is the target of the prediction. Maybe the best is to be in one of the cafés around it at coffee time, around 10-11 AM, and listen to their geek conversation or just watch their demeanor, which is probably similar to every other tech company in the world except for the fact that they go outside to have a coffee. Try to make out who are the executives, who are the commercial, who man customer supports, and who is in the basement manhandling the computers that make everything work or programming them.

And, while you are at it, you might see the signs for one such "Spiral startups", in another glass building, right by its side. You might even be able to watch it from outside the shuttered spaces, because it closed a while ago, signaling the onset of the bursting of the coworking bubble in Granada. Spiral Startups was, at one point in time, one of almost a couple of dozen coworking spaces in Granada. If you are not familiar with the concept, a coworking office is just an open space that provides a desk area, connectivity and amenities to freelancers and startup companies. During the crisis, they were a convenient and cheap alternative to either staying at your parents, renting real office space or crashing at a café. For less than 50€ a month, you could have your very own office to receive customers and interact with fellow entrepreneurs.

Only maybe it became too much of a good

thing. At the height of the phenomenon, there were more coworking spaces in Granada than in any other city in Spain, proving again that, when it comes to geekery, Granada rocks. After closing Spiral, other coworking spaces, like Cocorocó, also shut down, and then smaller ones. The only thriving space right now seems to be ErranT, which you are welcome to visit by itself or joining one of the many activities that take place there. It is actually very close to one of the biggest cibercafés that existed also in Granada in the late 90s and early aughts, Red Isis. It is now closed, as the rest of the public-access computer shops, of which there were quite a few in Granada. I have rarely been in such a kind of place in Granada, since the University provided us with Internet access at home since early one. However, there was one in every corner at the beginning of the century, before ADSL became affordable; it even resisted half a dozen of years, until now that we have Internet in our hand through our smartphones.

There might be still one open, plying mainly to migrants who use it mainly to call home, a crowd that is very different of the teens that crowded it back them to maim and kill through Unreal Tournament or other wargames.

Still, local cibercafés had something authentic in

them and were as much a showcase for local living culture as pubs or cemeteries, these later for living as well as dead culture, of course. The games played, the size and age of groups, the peek hours, were something to observe. I have been in cibercafés all over the world, and they are also a way of getting acquainted with the local keyboards, as well of being very jealous of security so as not to get your credentials stolen. It is rather safer now, with ubiquitous WiFi, although I would not put all my trust in an open network.

If you are not able to spot any Internet café, then, just look for your inner geek and grab your smartphone. Or maybe try one of the comic bookstores. Actually, one of the most venerable in Granada, Flash, is not so far away, by the end of San Antón street and actually pretty close to the rail relic we talked about in the chapter devoted to the train station. Its narrow storefront is jammed between a coffee and tea shop and a bakery, and you know you are in geek territory from the get go. As you enter through a narrow corridor, you will see right and left Warhammer 40K pieces for coloring and boxes. You will have to dodge or physically push people to advance past the new releases shelf and go around perusing Spanish and European comic, which are to the right and bottom of the library, or American and Japanese comic, to the left. Actually, it is a good occasion to browse Blacksad, the series of hardboiled graphic novels with a black cat as main character, beautifully drawn and scripted by Díaz Canales and Juanjo Guarnido, a local artist. Local fanzines are also for sale, and spontaneous discussion are started whenever a few of the usual visitors, of which there are quite a few, meet. This usually happens on Saturdays before closing at 2PM, so this is probably the best time to visit. You might end up with a few friends or maybe enemies, if you happen to like exactly the opposite of what passes as mainstream in the shop, usually American superhero stuff.

Flash is closed on Saturday afternoons, but Draco, the center of the local role playing games community, is not. Actually, there is kind of a gaming triangle that extends down to the end of the Alhamar street, where another shop, Shazam, used to be and if you allow a triangle to have another vertex, Dune used to be a few meters down Pedro Antonio. It is no longer there, and the options for gamers and comicateers have been greatly diminished, although they are well served, and probably will be for many years, with just Flash.

Or, if that fails, by any one of the many comic, anime and RPG-related events that take place almost monthly in Granada. There is a single ComiCon, but Granada boasts el Salón del Cómic, Japan Weekend, FicZone, Granada Gaming, with a delicious Retro Granada area with all kind of home computers and gaming consoles from the 80s and 90s, and which I really enjoyed, besides being able to check out all the local indie game creation scene.

> I am personally not too much into this kind of things, because lately they are more about cosplay and showing off than about talking or learning about comics and sequential art. However, since most people are attending K-Pop contests and karaoke fights, you might have the chance, as I did, to meet and greet comic creators and talk for a while with them, even if you had not heard about them before.

You can also be a hardcore geek of the kind that develops stuff and post it for everyone on GitHub. If that is the case and you never leave your laptop at home, I have just created Granada Geek in MeetUp, so that all groups, entrepreneurs, hacktivists, free software developers, and anyone, can create events for all to see. If it is not there it is probably not happening, but we expect to have something going on every week.

You can stop reading this and read your Blacksad. When you are done, keep reading this, there is so much more in Granada on and off the beaten track.

Or you can go and visit the Alhambra.

> You have done it already, right? You can now go back and do it again, but going off the beaten track. Is there a track not beaten to death in the Alhambra? Yes. Just look up, look at the patterns, and look at it with the eyes of mathematics.

Brush up your math first. Because to walk of the beaten track you need sturdy boots and math. Remember studying symmetry groups? I do not, either. Anyway, it is basically a way of covering a surface by picking up a motif, twisting, moving it, and flipping it. Get a black and white square, for instance. You copy/paste it and you have got two. Then turn it around clockwise, and you will have two squares with perpendicular motifs. You can keep and turning it until you get bored, and then copy the whole thing and flip it around. Well, whatever you do it, you can do it in 17 different ways: that is Fedorov's theorem, which was proposed by, you guessed it, Fedorov in 1891.

It is actually known as Fedorov-Schoenflies, or even Fedorov-Schoenflies-Bieberbach theorem. Actually the first two guys discovered it independently, because Fedorov did it first, but published it only in Russian and did not have Twitter and Google Translate for the world to know, so that other guy did it all over again. Third one generalized it to more dimensions. But the Alhambra is only three-dimensional in space, so we will not pay attention to the later.

Well, it so happens that the Alhambra is the only historical site, prior to Fedorov's theorem, that includes the 17 groups. Is that not incredible? Just go there and practice looking at the beautiful inlaid tiles. Look for a pattern: a colored 6- or 8-point star, an arabesque, whatever. Does it repeat itself? Is it flipped in the next group over? Does it rotate around? Take this guide and try to identify the different symmetry groups in the repetition patterns, or take some drawings home for reference.

Which is exactly what Maurits Cornelius Escher did, and did it twice. He visited the Alhambra twice: once in 1926 or 27, and the second time in 1936, three months before the Spanish Civil war. In fact, he had created tessellations, which are tilings of the surface, somewhat before that, in the early 20s, but, after his second visit, where he took detailed notes, he started to create his amazing "Metamorphoses", where one kind of tessellation, say, black and white squares, evolve into another, hexagons, going through gekkos and turtles and some mosaics that are, in fact, incredibly similar to what you find today in the Alhambra. He continued doing that kind of tilings mixing devils and angels, for instance, well into the 60s. And his inspiration was right here or maybe, right now, in front of you, in a humble set of majolica tiles in a 700 year old building.

As was the inspiration also for one of the local über-geeks: José Valdelomar or Val del Omar, widely unknown in Spain as well as elsewhere. In 1934, he created "Vibración de Granada", a short silent film that portraits the Alhambra and the whole city as a succession of short scenes that include fishes swimming in a fountain, reflections on the water and, at one time, a plane flying overhead. You can see a bit of David Lynch there, only 60 years prior to Twin Peaks. At the time, Valdelomar was involved with the "Pedagogic missions", itinerant workshops and shows created by the Republican Government; he was introduced to them by Federico García Lorca.

However, his geekery stems on his work on the machinery of the cinema. During the second world war, he registered a patent for what would now be called binaural sound. He wanted to create an integral experience with moviegoing, and in fact, the wrapping sound that is now implanted in many movie theaters was shown by him for the first time in a movie festival in Berlin in 1955. He experimented also with what is called now haptic perception, being thus a pioneer of video mapping.

However, he was ostracized, being ideologically contrary to the Franco regime. His work was discovered only after his death, with exhibitions in the national art museum and release of his work which, of course, can be enjoyed much better with the full sensory experience he favored. Although he went on to live in Madrid, he returns to Granada often and can be seen in these candid domestic videos. That is why you will not be able to see much of him, unless there is an exhibition. There is a Val del Omar room in the Parque de las Ciencias, and there is a Val del Omar prize for experimental cinema at the Young Cinematographers Festival in Granada. So let him live in your memory, or remember him when you watch Star Wars with surround sound.

THE GRAFFITI PNEUMONIA AND THE STREET ART FLU

One traveler once wrote about Granada: "It has a massive graffiti problem". Because it is true that you cannot walk a few steps without finding one way of street art or another in Granada. Street art is not concentrated in a few blocks, or even a neighborhood. It is all over the place, it is evident and, well, it is in occasions a nuisance. But in many more it is simply sublime. So, paraphrasing the famous rock and roll riff, Granada has got the graffiti pneumonia and the street art flu.

A quick primer on street art is in order here. Street art is anything created with artistic intent outdoors. So it goes from stickers to decorated walls in a parking. *Graffiti* is a subset made mainly with paint, usually spray. This one also goes in many different shapes: stencils are repetitive and done usually with a cookie-cutter pattern, tags are quick signature-like drafts, wild-style and throwups are more elaborated signatures, generally characteristic of a single street artist or *crew*, which is a collective, blockbusters cover a whole surface and finally *pieces* or *masterpieces* are elaborate paintings with a topic, that cover a wall or part of it and have many different colors and a recognizable topics. Other styles such as pastes are motifs painted on paper and that are stuck to walls, same as *skins* that are simply stickers, printed or painted name tags, you know, the ones with "Hello my name is…". Many other forms of street art are also possible, from contextual art that leverages preexisting shapes and colors in the surface it is made to tiles stuck on a wall through sculptures made with found art or *yarns*, fabric used to wrap trees and traffic signals.

One of the main things about Granada is that, not being a big city like London of New York, it is a showcase for all kinds of street art. A short route through a couple of neighborhoods will be enough to find most types of street art. That indicates also a thriving and vibrant art scene, with artists and crews developing their career from its inception as taggers or *bombers* to master pieces in *jams*, or long walls which are decorated by several artists or crews, mingling and mixing a masterpiece with the next.

And the main reason why it is so is probably sex. That is *Sex*, or also *El niño de las pinturas*, an incredibly talented *writer*, which started with a simple *sex* or *Sex69* tag you can still find everywhere and is now the main driving force of the street art *scene* nowadays. But together with him, several factors contribute to its dynamism. First one is its autonomy. Since there are so many artists and they have been able to develop a whole outdoor portfolio, they can live off their art, obviously not from the almost always free and spontaneous graffiti they throw everywhere, but from commissions either official or made by bars, restaurants or shop owners. This autonomy also means that it only depends on itself: it is not tied either to a political or urban activism group, skate or hip-hop crews or to urban exploration collectives. In fact, there is no UrbEx going on here that I know off, although it could obviously be underground and I could be none the wiser about it.

So it is difficult to say where to start, but since this is about going off the beaten track, ride the SN3 to the end of the line and start from there.

> You will be close to the Faculty of Fine Arts and the Computer Science and Telecommunications school. I talk about them on the chapters on the university of Granada and the one on geek stuff.

As soon as you step down from the bus, you will see a parking lot that is decorated with a graffiti version of Ronald McDonald, but that is only a small piece. Trace back your steps to the bus stop, go past the private academy and get to back of the motorway wall. From that place, almost a couple of kilometers of graffiti await you, mainly pieces and wild style, but some amazing stuff made by most of the writers in Granada in those days, a few years ago. You can recognize, for instance, *sendra*, or Ramón Sendra with his picture Samuel L. Jackson made with blobs of different colors. Also Nake, a young artist which is also an illustrator, or Rose, a German artist that blossomed in Granada. And also some pieces signed LJDA, *Los Jinetes del Apocalipsis*, the Apocalipsis riders the first collective created in the 90s and who are, still, active in some special occasions.

You will have a good idea of what to expect everywhere else in the city, but you will get a better idea if you proceed to the Faculty of Fine Arts. This will have to be on a weekday; due to budget cuts all the university is shuttered on weekends. Walk through the main gate through the roundabout and, forgetting about temporary expositions and cheap writing material which you should have checked out on its own chapter, make a right until you arrive to the big warehouse. You will already see graffiti from there: all that area is a showcase of graffiti made by Fine Arts students and by writers from elsewhere. And this is something that sets the graffiti scene in Granada apart from others: at its core there is a certain academic knowledge, but also the networks and communities that are created in this academic setting, as opposed to other scenes that coalesce around a particular neighborhood, the music of political activism scene. In fact, a Faculty of Fine Arts includes all of them: many stencils in town have been created as art projects by the students, and the fact that pieces, and not other kind of graffiti, are so prevalent in Granada is related to the formal studies that many of them have followed. You need an idea of composition, color, theme and many other things to create a piece, something that is not really needed to tag a wall or even to create a complex wild-style signature.

Many graffiti writers have studied there; many writers from elsewhere have at least followed a few courses here and, obversely, some students have dabbled with street art at least as a drunken caper some time in their life. Or maybe they have just worked in this extensive graffiti farm, where you see all kind of things: from *jams* created by several artists with aquatic motifs, to a utility closet fully decorated, to areas overgrown with weeds and with graffiti that have been overwritten with jokes by someone else. Also a wall decorated with representations of 1 euro coins. A black and red stencil with Darth Vader on a Holy Week float says "I am your father". Close to the wall, another utility has a shadow of a person smoking that seems to look at the rest of the graffiti imprinted in the same place. A bit to the right a squid holds a bleeding heart and says "squid love". And to the right of that, "Graffiti cannot be learned in class".

That might be true, but maybe the class as a collective spawns graffiti writers and helps them find their voice. That is interesting about this area: many graffiti writers cannot be found anywhere else in the city, or maybe in the world. Or, if you find them, they will have evolved to something different, probably better.

But let us travel to another place to check out the secret origins of graffiti in Granada. And you will have to take a ride or a bus to the other tip of the city to find out a bit more about them. In fact, you could follow the freeway for around fifteen kilometers, but it is better if you take a couple of buses and go to the Nuevo Los Cármenes stadium. Then look South, in the direction of the freeway, and will see a mostly dry river.

> That is the river Monachil, the third river in
> town and the one where 90% of the locals
> who you ask will fail.

Follow the river bed to get under the bridge
where the motorway crosses it. You will find a
jam that was created in the tenth anniversary of
the creation of LJDA. You cannot get more out
of the beaten track than that. There is fact no
track, just the compacted river bed. An
gorgeous graffiti depicting the four horsemen
and the inscription LJDA 10th anniversary. It
was painted in 2006, and celebrates 10 years of
creativity, generosity and chaos.

Sex-Raúl-Niño de las Pinturas himself tells, in an
interview in *Escenas del graffiti en Granada*,
how LJDA were born on a rainy Holy Week day
in 1996 by Juxa, Mobil, Shogun, Calahad and
himself, putting to good use 200 sprays they
brought, by bus, from Düsseldorf the day
before. The first wall was painted in Cervantes
avenue. That wall has disappeared, and I have
not been able to find anything about it, so it is
not worth the while that you walk there, but it
is interesting to check out Yerma street.

> Yerma is the name of a play by Federico
> García Lorca. Meaning laid to waste or

> infertile, it is metaphorically applied to a woman. And it is a paradox that this street spawned such a fertile art.

This street is where Calahad and Sex lived in the early 90s, and is covered in one of the sides by a brick wall. The first graffiti were simple tags that read Sex or Calahad, and they were accompanied by others, spirit, spit... The first pieces, already in 94, made by Spit and others, already show the compressed evolution of the artistic career that starts with a single black spray and a fast tag and progresses to increasingly complex pieces, the state we are seeing today.

> This street is very close to the Instituto de Astrofísica de Andalucía, one of the stops in the geek route. Besides, around the corner there is a graffiti wall with a astronomic theme. Check it out too.

However, you will see only those twenty years old graffiti as parts of the palimpsest that Yerma street is now. It is still painted, and some pieces are quite old, but the piece by el Niño de las Pinturas that celebrates the street itself is in the middle, it features a bar code and black and white motifs. Just walk up and down and let the city talk to you, and return later on to see what has happened. Graffiti are alive, and sometimes writers *bomb* other writers by writing over them, although there is a hierarchy of respect: pieces over wildstyle over throwups over tags. And nobody, ever, will write over anything done by El Niño de las Pinturas.

Walk down Camino Bajo de Huétor and you will get to the wall where the inscription "Ana Mari, do you want to watch Star Wars with me" was written. It is the quintessential graffiti, and it also goes across the lines of the geek culture that we love so much in Granada. It went viral, getting to a list of the 17 best ways to say "I love you" in a wall. It eventually disappeared, being the wall of a private home and not a construction site or some official place. Love is forever, but declarations are, and maybe should be, ephemeral.

> Another inscription, "Argentina and me, a super-logic love", also in Granada and written in the back of the Müller palace at the north tip of the Gran Vía, made it to this list too. We might meet it in our graffiti wanderings, so I will just mention it right here.

From there, you can walk straight ahead to the wall of the Escolapios school, in the Callejón del Pretorio.

> This school is still active. José Val del Omar, mentioned in the geek chapter, studied here.

This wall contains one of the oldest graffiti that still exist in Granada. Some parts of it were created in 1993, a graffiti called "Dragons" and drawn by Spirit and Chapas, but painting continued in the next year and, even today, the wall is completely covered with beautiful pieces and wild-style tags, although probably none of the originals persist; they are just tiny layers of color in the surface of the wall. This wall might be a result of a technique that graffiti writers mentioned and that might have been used elsewhere: drop *bombs* on a wall and make it ugly, do it by night and unnoticed. Later on, when that wears and the wall looks like a showcase of urban decay, talk to the owner and ask for permission to do a beautiful piece, which you do. So this was, in fact, <u>authorized and even documented by the local daily, which provided some sprays</u>.

This piece is, in fact, beautiful, and current instance includes Sex, Nake and many others, including Drew. But the part I like the most is more or less in the middle and uses the *trompe l'oeil* technique to simulate a chasm opening in the wall with a figure with elongated arms grabbing another graffiti to avoid falling. It was created by XNOS, which has a few other pieces to his name, but he is not so well known by this name, unlike the signatures to the right, Sex, Rakis and even LJDA again are still there. Rakis was born in Düsseldorf and was the one in charge of bringing sprays to the whole LJDA crew. He continues collaborating to this day, with his wildstyle signatures that blend with the beautiful pieces by Sex. And in fact, XNOS is also known as Pornostars, which included people like Reno, Drew and writers from other places like Kies. In fact, either as XNOS or as Pornostars they have been going places and decorating walls all over Europe.

But let us go across the river, to Granada. For a long time, the residents in this part of the city said "I am going to Granada" every time they walked to the city center. But, in fact, we are in a different neighborhood, different rules.

But the same graffiti. The *Virgen"* *neighborhood, smack in the city center, features* *stencils, pastes and many faces drawn by Sex.* *Raúl was probably the first one to be considered* all city* that is, a person that has covered all corners or neighborhoods of the city. From the Chana to the Zaidín, through the city center, there are few blocks where el Niño de las

Pinturas has not left his particular signature, with brown hues, beautiful faces and cogs or machinery pieces that appear everywhere in his work.

However, it is el Realejo neighborhood where he is really prolific and the place we have to walk over and over again to check whatever new he has concocted in his mind. Or in other cases what has disappeared, like this amazing cat that appeared in January 2015 and that promptly was taken down due to a protest by the neighbors, who said it did not keep the style of the rest of the houses. Which is blatantly false, since the style of this particular zone is *defined* by graffiti.

Just wander around every single alley and street and you will find things to contemplate, but there is a blind alley, called Parra de San Cecilio, and which is right behind the San Cecilio church

> Which is also a decaying exhibition of *trompe l'oeil*.

and one of the places which you *cannot* visit using Google Street Maps, that is why you will have to go there and be there physically.

You will be glad you did it. On the left hand side, or in front, depending on how you came in, you will see first a piece with an intriguing woman and "Las palabras se perderán sin remedio", "The words will be lost without a solution" combined with trees and geometric drawings, and it continues, with a yellow background, for a hundred meters with all kinds of colors and styles, with ghosts, Urquell the TV star and a checker board, all linked by irregular tessellations. You can also look at the other side, although the work is minor and changes from time to time. But get to the end, where a skull awaits you.

This skull is a great example of contextual art. The teeth, nose stub and eyes are part of the building. It is only black paint applied to make the silhouette of the skull pop out by itself. This was the basement of the Colombia hotel and restaurant, which is abandoned and derelict, so it is kind of an epitaph too.

Walk back down and let us get to the end of the tour. Although, as Val del Omar finished his motion pictures, there is "No end" for graffiti in Granada, even as vandalism sometimes forces crackdowns on what is only a form of artistic expression. Get to the corner between Escoriaza and Calle Molinos, to the recently named Joe Strummer square.

This is one of the few places I will not have

to add words to the dictionary for. And it is named for a person, the leader of The Clash, that actually lived in Granada for a time. It has been there since 2013, and inaugurated with a concert which I attended and who had the drummer boy for the Clash actually playing. It was a wonderful experience.

In a radius of 50 meters from the decaying face of Strummer, made by none other than Sex, several dozens of square meters of the finest graffiti look at you, most made by Sex himself. The little square to the right includes a whole house and the husk of another decorated with browns and beiges and tan. It is nice to watch in spring, because the golden sun inundates it all, it is incredible to watch in fall and winter, because the naked branches of the tree will give you full sight of this incredible corner.

But from there you will see uphill a wall that is decorated up a down, in a blockbuster that is actually a piece with a kid, a kid that asks questions, and further up the street, a two-story house painted red, with a baby on it, and street art all over: a broken TV turned into an sculpture, and even the little wall that prevents you from falling over painted with the skyline of the Alhambra.

And that is the beginning of the Barranco del Abogado, which deserves another chapter. You are also a few meters from the Fives-Lille steam engine and the "fake engineer" Ricardo de la Cierva street, referenced in the geekery chapter.

From there, remember that Granada is a living graffiti jewel. And the perfect recipe for finding them is just walking off the beaten track. Just like the rest of the book.

EPILOGUE

Books are never finished. This book even more so. I will continue changing it with your feedback and whatever new chapters I think about in my wanderings and workings in Granada. Your Kindle will kindly update your copy once it's uploaded by me. If you have a hard copy, and I will email you updates in epub or Kindle format, whatever you prefer.

ABOUT THE AUTHOR

Just a guy who writes stuff and lives in Granada. Can be reached at... well, you know the drill. Use Google. Even email addresses are not for ever.

15988467R00062

Printed in Great Britain
by Amazon